The (Little) Book of Love

The Story of God and You

**With God's Love
from the
Presbyterian Church of Marion
Marion Center, PA**

Rod Pinder

Dedicated to Mike Fleetwood

who mentored me in sharing God's Love.

CONTENTS

PREFACE

People love a love story – especially when they're a part of it. You're about to read the greatest love story ever told, and it's partly about you. This is a story about you and the greatest lover who ever lived. I'm talking, of course, about God.

It's no secret that God loves you. You've heard that countless times. You may or may not have believed it, but it is true. In fact, it is really the most important truth in your life. As we explore this love story, I think its importance and truth will thrill you more than a high school crush.

Chapter 1

Made for Love

Our love story starts before you were even born. In fact, it started before time began. God Himself tells us so. The Bible is God's Word. It's a collection of the most important things God has said to His people since the very beginning. And in the Bible, we find these words. *The LORD appeared to us in the past saying, I have loved you with an everlasting love; I have drawn you with loving-kindness.* (Jeremiah 31:3)

Takes your breath away, doesn't it? The

wisest, most powerful, most beautiful and most loving Being in the universe loves you. You. He always has, and He always will. That's the way it is with an everlasting love.

As a matter of fact, that's why God created you. God made you for a loving relationship with Himself. You were designed to love God, because God loves you. In Psalm 100:3 the Bible says, *Know that the LORD is God. It is He who made us, and we are His; we are His people, the sheep of His pasture.*

Everyone wants to know the meaning of life. "Why am I here?" is the quintessential question. Nowadays, people are taught that human beings are the random result of a chain of cosmic accidents. You just sort of happened to evolve, lucky you. Originally you were nothing more than primordial slime.

If that's true, however, life really can't have any intrinsic meaning, value, or purpose. This pointless point of view is shared and expressed by people as diverse as the

Existentialist Philosophers and the Hip Hop artists who sang, "You and me, baby, ain't nothin' but mammals, so let's do it like they do it on the Discovery Channel."[1] What a depressing lie!

The truth is that you are not an accident, you're a work of art. You're a masterpiece! Your Creator custom-made you for a very important purpose: to love Him. You were made to love God.

> **You were made to love God.**

Once, there was a brilliant young man who spent his life searching for life's meaning in cults and culture and sexual escapades. But he never found what he was looking for in those things. In his middle years, this man tuned to Christ and, after a while, became a bishop. We know him as St. Augustine. Augustine started his autobiography with

---

[1] Bloodhound Gang "The Bad Touch" 1999
[2] Extreme, "Hole Hearted" 1991

these marvelous words to God, "You awaken us to delight in praising You, for You have made us for yourself, and our hearts are restless 'til they find rest in You." (*Confessions* of St. Augustine, Book I.)

God has made us for Himself, and our hearts are restless until they find rest in Him. Someone has said that there is a God-shaped vacuum in each of us. To put it in the words of the 1990's rock song, "There's a hole in my heart that can only be filled by you."[2]

Like young Augustine, people try to fill that vacuum with all manner of things, some lofty and some loathsome. But none of them fully satisfies. Nothing else can fill the God-shaped hole. And so, our love story takes a tragic turn.

---

[2] Extreme, "Hole Hearted" 1991

Chapter 2
Unrequited Love

The tragedy of our love story is that, though God has loved us with an everlasting love, we haven't loved Him in return. Not completely. Not the way we were designed to love. Many people are fond of God, but they keep Him in the "friend zone." They're not willing to commit their lives to Him the way He is committed to you and me. Even though this perfectly wise God who loves us with an everlasting love has told us how to live life to the fullest, people want to live

7

their lives their way, not God's way. This is what the Bible calls sin.

And here's the thing about sin. Sin separates us from God's love. Sin is unfaithfulness. Sin is cheating on the God who loves us.

When most people hear the word "sin" they think of gross misconduct: murder, robbery, adultery, bigotry. No doubt about it, those things are certainly sin. But according to the Bible, God's understanding of sin is deeper, wider, broader. We sin every time we let anything come between us and God. Anytime. Anything, great or small.

> Sin seprates us from God's love

A profound, ancient prayer powerfully expresses the scope of sin. It says, "I confess to God the Almighty, and to you, my brothers and sisters, I have sinned. In my thoughts and in my words, in the things that

I have done and in what I have failed to do, I have sinned."

You see, sin isn't just about the things we do. Sin also includes the things we say and the things we think, our attitudes. It even includes our negligence to do or say or even think the right thing when we have the opportunity.

All of this is sin. All of this is what keeps us from living in the loving relationship with God that He created us to enjoy. And no one is exempt. No one is perfect in what he or she does, says, thinks or fails to do. We have all cheated on the God who loves us.

The Bible hits the nail on the head when it says, *If we claim to be without sin, we deceive ourselves and the truth is not in us.* (1 John 1:8)

The greatest love story ever told includes a break-up. And it's our fault, not God's. But thank the Lord, the story doesn't have to end there.

Chapter 3

The World's Greatest Lover

We must understand that God doesn't need us. He got along fine before we were born. God is perfectly happy being God. Nevertheless, God loves you with an everlasting love. So, God isn't willing just to let you go. He wants you back. He loves you so much, He thinks you are to die for.

And so, He did.

1 John 4:10 says, *This is love: not that we loved God, but that He loved us and sent His*

son as an atoning sacrifice for our sins.

What astonishing love! God loves us so
much that He sent His Son to take away our
sins – that's what an atoning sacrifice does.
It takes away sin. So, when God's Son,
Jesus Christ, died on the cross, He was
taking away our sin. He was removing the
barrier between us and the Father, so that
our loving relationship with Him could be
restored. Because Jesus came as an atoning
sacrifice, to take away our sin, we can live
in God's love, just as we were designed to
do. The God-shaped vacuum can be filled.

But this love is even greater than it sounds
from that verse alone. To understand it fully,
we need to know just who Jesus Christ is.
Jesus Christ is God Himself in human form.
The Bible teaches this in many places. For
example, Jesus said things like, *"I and the
Father are one"* (John 10:30) and, *"Anyone
who has seen me has seen the Father"* (John
14:19). Jesus is fully God and fully human.

I have a son. He is a fine, godly man and I

am very proud of him. I even admire him. But he is not me. He is a different person. God's Son, on the other hand, is God. Of course! God is Father, Son and Holy Spirit.

If I were to send my son on a mission, maybe to buy milk or something, he would go, but I wouldn't. By contrast, when God, the Father, sends His Son, it is God Himself who goes.

This means that when God sent His Son to become the sacrifice for our sins, God was really sacrificing Himself, not someone else. It was God who suffered on the cross. It was God who bled. It was God who cried. It was God Himself who tasted death.

And why did God do this? To win you back. God loves you with an everlasting love. So, no price is too high for Him to pay in order to have you with Him. He would do anything to shower you with His love. In fact, He already has.

In Jesus Christ, God became a man. He told us about God's love. He showed us what it looks like to live in God's love. To use an old-fashioned word, He came to woo us back to God. Then, in order to remove the sin-barrier that separated us from Him, Jesus sacrificed His life. The sacrifice of Jesus

The sacrifice of Jesus Christ takes away our sin and restores us in God's love.

Christ takes away our sin and restores us in God's love.

Jesus Christ is, beyond doubt, the world's greatest lover. And He loves you. So, what are you going to do about that amazing, astonishing love? How will you respond?

Chapter 4

To Love Him is to Trust Him

In the early 1970s there were a couple of famous and popular Broadway shows about the life of Christ. One of them was *Jesus Christ Superstar*. Superstar was not so much a statement, but a penetrating and well posed question. It wasn't written by a Christian but by a seeker who wanted to understand who Jesus Christ was and is. It is a powerful play.

To my tastes, the most beautiful and haunting song from that play was sung by Mary Magdalene, a woman who had been a prostitute but then came to know Jesus. Wrestling with the contrast between His love and her sin, she sings, "I don't know how to love Him."[3]

That's the question, isn't it? If He loves us so much, how shall we love Him?

Thankfully, Jesus Himself answers that question. In John 14:15 Jesus says, *"If you love me, you will obey what I command."* Well that makes sense, doesn't it? When we love someone, we do things he or she likes. We try to carry out his or her wishes. And what is it that Jesus wants from us? How do we do what He wants? The Bible tells us that, too. 1 John 3:23 says, *And this is his command: to believe in the name of his Son, Jesus Christ, and to love one another as he commanded us.*

---

[3] Weber, Andrew Lloyd and Rice, Tim "I Don't Know How to Love Him" 1970

One essential way we respond to God's love is to believe in Jesus. (The second way is to love one another, but we'll talk about that later.) That, of course, raises another question: What does it mean to believe in Him? Many people misunderstand the meaning of "believe."

The word "believe" has different definitions. For example, if I say I believe in Bigfoot or UFOs, you know I'm saying I think they exist. Some people believe in these things and some people don't, just as some people believe in Jesus and others don't.

However, if I say I believe in my wife, that's a different kind of statement, isn't it? It would be ridiculous for me to inform you that I think my wife exists. I can prove it easily enough by introducing her to you. No, when I say I believe in my wife, I mean I think she intends good for me. I mean I think she is capable and competent. In short, I mean I trust her.

That's closer to what the Bible means when

it talks about believing in Jesus. It doesn't mean merely to think He exists – though He certainly does. It doesn't simply mean to agree that He is fully God and fully human, that He was born of a Virgin, worked miracles and healings, gave his life to take away our sin, rose from the dead, sent the Holy Spirit, and is coming again. All that is true enough, but to believe in Jesus Christ means to trust Him.

To trust Jesus means to count on Him as your Savior. It means to trust that His loving sacrifice on the cross really does take away your sins. *You* really are forgiven. You really are *forgiven.* It means to trust that, because of this, you now live in the Father's love. The break-up is over. You and God are reunited through Christ. Those things are true, but they don't do you any good unless you believe them from your heart. They only apply to you when you trust Him.

People want to trust many things to restore their relationship with God. Mostly they want to try to be good enough to make things up to God. They try to be good and hope the good outweighs the bad. But how much good would it take to blot out our betrayal of the One who loves us with an everlasting love? We can't be good enough. We can't make it up to Him. So, if we trust in ourselves, we're bound to fail. But we don't have to trust ourselves. Christ has us covered. And when we trust Him, who gave His life for us, our sins are forgiven. The barrier that separated us from God is shattered and we are restored.

That isn't all, however. To believe in Jesus means not only that we trust him for forgiveness of our sins, it also means we trust Him with the way we live our day to day lives. What He says goes. In other words, we trust Him as Lord.

Suppose I told you it was going to rain. If you believe me, you'll carry an umbrella. Suppose I tell you about great food at a certain restaurant. If you believe me, you'll go there to eat. Suppose I told you that a certain stock was going triple in value two weeks from today. What would you do? If you don't believe me at all, you won't invest a penny. If you believe me "kinda sorta," you might put a few extra dollars on that commodity. If you truly trust me, however, you'll pour every cent you can get into that stock. Mortgage the house. Sell the car. Take out a loan. Invest all you can, because you believe the payoff is going to be fantastic. Someone you trust said so.

We receive God's love by trusting in Christ

When we trust Jesus, we do what He says, we follow His teachings. We're willing to invest everything we have – our talents, our time, our careers, our relationships – in doing what He says.

To believe in Jesus means to trust Him. And when we believe in Jesus, our love relationship with God is restored. That's why the Bible says, *Yet to all who received him, to those who believed in his name, he gave the right to become children of God.* (John 1:12)

We receive God's love by trusting in Christ. But putting our trust in Jesus isn't the end point. It's only the beginning.

Chapter 5

A Life of Love

Once we receive God's love by putting our trust in Jesus Christ, we start to change. We begin to become more and more like the One who loves us. Specifically, we begin to love the way He loves.

That makes perfect sense. 1 John 4:19 puts it this way. *We love because He first loved us.*

Jesus Himself said that being one of His followers was about living a life of love. When someone asked Him, what was the most important thing about living the way God designed us to live, *Jesus replied: "'Love the Lord your God with all your heart and with all your soul and with all your mind.' This is the first and greatest commandment. And the second is like it: 'Love your neighbor as yourself.' All the Law and the Prophets hang on these two commandments."* (Matthew 22: 37-40)

But what does that look like? How do we love God and love our neighbors? Answers to that question could fill a whole book, and still be incomplete.[4] But we can look at a few highlights.

We love God by worshiping and obeying Him. We love God by praying – not just telling God what we want but asking God what He wants and trying to cooperate with

---

[4] See Pinder, Rod *The Book of Love: Seven Words to Transform Your World* (Coming in 2020. See pages 26-34 below.)

Him. We love God by reading the Bible.[5]
The Bible is like one huge love letter from
the world's greatest lover. The Bible is like
an owner's manual from the One who
designed us to live in His love. We love God
by being baptized and taking Communion.
We love God by allowing Him to guide our
thoughts, our words and our actions. That's
just skimming the surface, but you get the
idea.

And what about loving other people? How
do we do that? Again, the answer is more
than we can
unpack right
now, but it
includes things
like service,
kindness, generosity. Especially it includes
telling others what I've been telling you. It
means sharing the Good News of God's love
in Jesus Christ.

We follow Jesus in a life of love.

---

[5] See Pinder, Rod *Nasty Rumors: Can You Believe What
They're Saying about the Bible* © 2019 Rod Pinder (See
pages 35-39 below.)

About 1,000 years ago, St. Thomas Aquinas suggested that to love someone is to will his or her highest good.[6] That's not bad. Love isn't always easy. Love isn't always indulgent. Sometimes love is hard. But love is our purpose. Love is why we were created. And so, we follow Jesus in a life of love.

One more thing. It's impossible for us to love the way Jesus loves by our own strength. We're still too weak. We're still too selfish. We still get distracted. But here's a beautiful truth. God doesn't expect us to do this in our own strength. Instead, God wants us to let His love flow through us. We're not supposed to manufacture our own love, we're supposed to be conduits, letting Him

> God wants us to let His love flow through us.

---

[6] Aquinas, Thomas, *Summa Theologica II II 26*

pour His love into us so that it gushes out onto others.

Romans 5:5 says, *And hope does not disappoint us, because God has poured out his love into our hearts by the Holy Spirit, whom he has given us.*

Can you imagine a more exciting life than that? To follow Jesus in a life of love means we let the very love of God flow through us and splash out on everyone we meet. That kind of love will change our lives. It will change the lives of those around us. Eventually, that kind of love will change the world.

Chapter 6
Happily Ever After

Now, a good love story ought to have a happy ending, don't you think? But not this love story. This love story doesn't have any ending at all!

John 3:16 says, *For God so loved the world that He gave His one and only Son, that whoever believes in Him shall not perish but have eternal life.*

When Jesus died on the cross, He took away our sin. But He wasn't finished yet. On the third day God raised Jesus from the dead. He conquered death itself! So those who trust in Jesus receive not only the forgiveness of their sins, they also receive eternal life!

The Bible teaches that when we die our spirits go to heaven to be with Jesus. We will remain in heaven with Him until He comes again. One day He will return to earth, destroy all evil and establish His kingdom of perfect love in a new heaven and a new earth. And we will live there with Him forever. Happily, ever after. Those who trust in Jesus inherit eternal life, basking in everlasting love.

> Those who trust in Jesus inherit eternal life, basking in everlasting love.

Isn't that a great love story? As I said, it's the greatest love story ever told. Is it your love story? It can be. It will be your love story when you invite Jesus Christ to come into your life, take away the sin barrier that separates you from God and help you live a life of love, now and forever. In other words, it will be your love story when you put your trust in Jesus Christ. One way you might do that is by sincerely praying the following prayer.

Dear Father, thank You for loving me with an everlasting love and for creating me to love You. I confess that I have sinned by ignoring Your love and by living life my way instead of Yours. Thank You for sending Jesus to take away my sin and restore me in Your perfect love. I put my trust in Him and ask You to pour the Holy Spirit into my heart. Help me to live a life of love, now, and for eternity. I ask in Jesus' name. Amen.

My prayer for you is that you will grow in God's love through Christ for the rest of your life. I encourage you to find Bible-believing friends to love, encourage and support you as you grow. I also invite you email me at PastorRodPinder@gmail.com and to visit www.PastorRodPinder.com regularly for more resources.

Additional copies of *The Little Book of Love* are available at Amazon.com .

Additional Resources

Coming in 2020

The Book of Love
Seven Words to Transform Your World

Rod Pinder

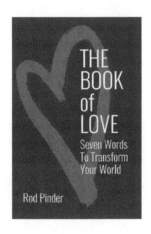

Have you ever asked any of these crucial questions?

> ➢ How can I enjoy **better relationships**?
> ➢ What gives life **meaning and purpose**?
> ➢ Where can I find a **sense of belonging**?

- ➢ How can I help **make the world a better place**?
- ➢ What role should **material possessions** play in my life?
- ➢ What happens **when I die**?

Sound and profound answers to these and similar questions are freely available, but they're in the last place many people think to look. Yet one powerful verse of the Bible addresses these and other issues with life-transforming wisdom that is both simple and sublime. Discover these rich insights in *The Book of Love: Seven Words to Transform Your World* by Rod Pinder.

The Book of Love expands on the truths found in this booklet, *The (Little) Book of Love,* and applies them to everyday life in an understandable, enjoyable, and comprehensive way. If you like what you just read, *The Book of Love* is for you!

Watch www.PastorRodPinder.com for updates and details.

Introducing

The Book of Love
Seven Words to Transform Your World

[Sample]

By Rod Pinder

Lost and Found

I still have to laugh at myself when I think about it. Four people spent forty-five minutes each trying to find my car keys after an evening Bible study at our church. We looked everywhere – twice. We checked my study, the classroom, the worship area, the bathrooms, my car, *everywhere*. We stopped, scratched our heads and searched some more. I *had* to find those keys. Where could they possibly be?

Finally, somebody spied them. They were lying on my briefcase by the main entrance. I had put them there before class to remind me to take care of some small detail before I went home. The keys I needed weren't lost at all. In fact, they had been in plain sight during the entire search! I had just forgotten where I had left them.

Have you ever "lost" something very important, only to find it in the most obvious of places? Many of us have searched for eyeglasses that were perched on our foreheads, or hunted for a piece of paper we had tucked into a pocket, or finally found our shoes on the shoe rack. Nearly everyone has had the experience of discovering some "lost" treasure that was right where it belonged the whole time. We simply forgot where we left the thing.

Crucial Questions

In the same way, people in our world have lost the answers to some very important questions. Have you ever asked yourself about any of these pressing issues?

"How can I have better relationships?" Relationships are core to our lives. Family, friendship, romance. Maybe you'd like to improve your relationship with your children or parents, your boss or co-workers, your customers, your students, your teachers, neighbors or friends. Maybe you feel a need to go deeper in your relationship with your husband or wife or boyfriend or girlfriend.

Or maybe you've asked, "How can I do the right thing" in the moral sense of the word? Which actions are morally right? Is there even such a thing as right and wrong? Should you obey a certain set of rules? Should you do those things that will bring about the best consequences? And does that mean the best consequences for you? Or for the majority? Or for someone else? Maybe you should mind mama's maxim and ask, "What if everybody did that?" Or follow the slacker slogan, "If it feels good, do it."

And if you're not always sure of what the right thig is, then you may have asked, "How do I deal with guilt?"

Or, let's go for the biggie, the quintessential question, "What is the purpose of life?" Why are we all here in the first place?

And there are more questions. Big questions. Basic questions.

"Where can I find a sense of belonging?"

"How can I help make the world a better place?"

"What role should material possessions play in my life?"

"What happens when I die?"

Such questions haunt us and hound us and send us scurrying for answers.

These are among the very issues that have occupied many of the brightest minds in human history. And no wonder. Think how much richer life might be if we could only find the solutions to these puzzles. Imagine the joy, the confidence, the peace that the knowledge of such truths could produce in us! Our hearts pine for answers to these crucial questions. From the mystical to the mundane there are things we long to know that will help our lives be more meaningful, beautiful, abundant.

Could it be that we have not really lost these key truths at all? Is it possible that the answers we need are waiting to be discovered in the most obvious of places? Right where they belong? Right where we left them?

Seven Words to Transform Your World

What would you think if I told you that

you could find stimulating and satisfying answers to those questions and countless more in one exquisite Bible verse? What if I shared with you seven simple words that speak powerfully and profoundly to all those questions, all those longings? Seven words that can change your life? Seven words that could transform your world? Would you like to hear them? Would you like to learn them? Would you like to build your life around them? I think you will.

This one verse is simple, yet sublime. It's an axiomatic statement, a burst of light that radiates illumination on our darkest mysteries. When we apply this foundational truth to our daily lives, answers to our crucial questions begin to emerge. Joyous, surprising, meaningful, world-shaping answers are suggested in those seven words. *The Book of Love: Seven Words to Transform Your World* unpacks and helps us understand that single, breath-taking verse.

Also by Rod Pinder

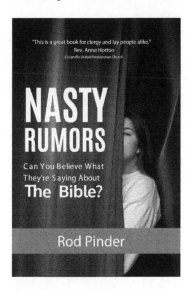

Nasty Rumors
Can You Believe What They're Saying about the Bible?

Have you heard any of this scuttlebutt?

- ➢ **The Bible is too old** to be relevant today.
- ➢ **The Bible cannot be trusted** because we no longer have the original manuscripts.

- The Bible's original message has been **lost in translation.**
- The Bible is **too hard to understand.**
- What about the **"Lost Books of the Bible?"**
- The Bible is **just another religious book.**

In *Nasty Rumors: Can You Believe What They're Saying about the Bible?* Dr. Rod Pinder brings pastoral concern, scholarly insight, faith-filled devotional wisdom, and delightful humor to bear as he examines and refutes these and other *Nasty Rumors* about the Christian Scriptures.

Available in paperback and on Kindle at Amazon.com

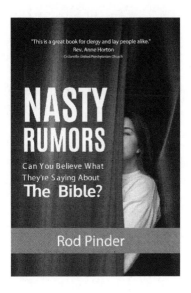

What People Are Saying about

Nasty Rumors

Reading *Nasty Rumors: Can You Believe What They're Saying about the Bible?* was a truly transformative experience. It is insightful, engaging, and answers so many questions I have had about the history, origin and authenticity of the Bible. I could feel the Holy Spirit moving as I read. This book has re-ignited my desire to dig into the Word and to live my faith out daily. It is scholarly and well researched, while also fun and entertaining to read. I found myself not wanting to put it down. If you have ever wondered how we can know if the Bible is truly inspired by God, or if it has been accurately transcribed and translated through the years, this book answers those questions and more. It is a captivating read in whatever stage you are in Faith, and I highly recommend it.

- Kathryn Matos, MPA, Assistant to the City Manager,
  Sunny Ilses Beach, FL

"Nasty Rumors is a wonderful combination of insightful reasoning, clear arguments, and rich, personal warmth. The book address real questions Christians have about the reliability of the source book of our faith,

providing clear, persuasive answers along with wise, practical advice for bringing the truth of the Bible to bear on the life of all who seek to follow Jesus. This is a book that I, as a pastor and teacher of the Bible, will strive to get into the hands of all the members of my flock."

- Rev. Gary Chorpenning, Pastor, Venice Presbyterian Church near Pittsburgh,PA Writer at https://gachorpenning.com

Nasty Rumors is a gem of a volume. Written thoughtfully and with humor and humility, it provides helpful encouragement for those who have written the Faith off because they have believed the *rumors*.

- Steve Strickler, Teaching Elder, Evangelical Presbyterian Church

This is a great book for clergy and lay people alike. Rod uses great illustrations, humor, and solid Biblical content as he dispels various myths we have heard about the Bible. His explanations are thorough but very relatable.

- Rev. Anne Horton, Cedarville United Presbyterian Church, Ceaderville, OH

Pastor Rod's book *Nasty Rumors*, although targeted for believers, is a great mix of apologetics and church history that would be convincing even to the critic that Scripture can be trusted as a reliable source. Rod has done the work, the research, and put together a wonderful read for not only the people in the pews but the church leaders among us as well. The material found here serves as a wonderful aid in our quest to bring the Good News to a hurting world that questions the validity of the Scriptures we hold as our final rule of faith and practice.

- John A. Terech Jr. Ex Dir of Operations ECO: A Covenant Order of Evangelical Presbyterians

Future books by Rod Pinder include:

Preaching in the Power of the Holy Spirit
How God's Word Creates Reality

The Joseph Curve
How God Fulfils Vision

Kill the Old Man (It's an Inside Job)
How to Die to Self and Grow in Christ-likeness

Tiptoe through the T.U.L.I.P.
A Moderate Look at Modern Calvinism

For updates, videos, blogs and more information, visit www.PastorRodPinder.com

ABOUT THE AUTHOR

Helping people grow in God's love in Jesus Christ is Rod Pinder's passion and mission in life. It's one thing that gets his blood pumping. Through preaching, teaching, writing, music and videos, Rod has shared that love on every continent except Australia and Antarctica (so far). Having served as a pastor for more than thirty-six years, Dr. Pinder has retired from pastoral ministry. He continues to share God's love with people through books, blogs, public speaking, videos, and is planning to start a podcast. Follow him at www.PastorRodPinder.com or Pastor Rod on Facebook and YouTube.

Made in the USA
Monee, IL
05 February 2020